Mindfulness for Beginners

How to Live in The Present, Stress and Anxiety Free

The information herein is offered for informational purposes solely, and is universal as so. The presentation of the information is without contract or any type of guarantee assurance.

The trademarks that are used are without any consent, and the publication of the trademark is without permission or backing by the trademark owner. All trademarks and brands within this book are for clarifying purposes only and are the owned by the owners themselves, not affiliated with this document.

Table of Contents

Introduction   v

Chapter 1: What Mindfulness Is and What It Is Not   2

Chapter 2: Why Bother with Mindfulness/ Meditation   6

Chapter 3: It's All in Your Head   8

Chapter 4: Be Mindful of What You Put Into Your Body and Mind   12

Chapter 5: Eat and Drink Slow   14

Chapter 6: Tips for Beginners   16

Chapter 7: How to Practice Mindfulness   18

Chapter 8: How to Live in the Present   22

Chapter 9: How to Become Stress and Anxiety Free   24

Chapter 10: How to Make a Plan to Meditate Mindfully   28

Chapter 11: Letting Go of Your Past   30

Chapter 12: Take Small Steps in the Right Direction, Everyday   32

Chapter 13: Be Present, Compassionate, and Grateful When Talking to Others   36

Chapter 14: Let Go of Distractions   38

Chapter 15: Mindfulness at Home and Work   40

Conclusion   44

Introduction

I want to thank you and congratulate you for reading the book, *Mindfulness for Beginners: How to Live in The Present, Stress and Anxiety Free.*

Life is full of stress, and these days, it's so easy to fall into the traps of depression and anxiety. When that happens, you might feel like your life right now isn't good at all—and that you'd rather go back to the past because it's where your happiness lies.

That way of thinking is wrong. In fact, there are so many things you could do to help you forget about your worries, live in the present, and let go of anxiety and stress. You can start taking care of your mind—and mindfulness is a good start.

By reading this book, you will learn more about mindfulness, understand what mindfulness is about, why it's important, why eating and drinking slow is important, how you can live a life free of stress and anxiety—and so much more!

Read this book now and find out how.

I hope you enjoy it!

Mindfulness for Beginners

Chapter 1: What Mindfulness Is and What It Is Not

Before anything else, what is mindfulness really about? And what it is not?

Mindfulness is...

To put it simply, mindfulness is about focusing on one's thoughts, emotions, and sensations without judgment, with intent, and with full acceptance. It has Buddhist roots, most especially *Sati*, which is part of the *7 Factors of Enlightenment*. According to tradition, Sati is a way to recognize the *dhammas*, which are both reality and phenomena. When this is achieved, a person is well on his way to *Nirvana*, or a state of total serenity and happiness.

It was then popularized in America and other parts of the world by Jon Kabat-Zinn, the creator of the Stress Reduction Clinic, and a well-known Professor Emeritus. He then created the *Mindfulness Based Stress Reduction Technique*, which aims to help people recognize their problems, not to wallow in them, but to actually exorcise them from their lives. Mindfulness is then believed to have a lot to do with the reduction of stress and anxiety.

In fact, a number of psychological and psychiatric facilities all over the world have been developing various techniques of mindfulness to help people undergoing therapy. In a way, they believe that science and meditation could actually go together, and bring some good in the world.

Clinical psychologists have said that the main reason why mindfulness is beneficial is because of the so-called two-component model. The said model is all about:

1. Self-Regulation, or how a person gets to control his attentiveness and gets to focus attention on his immediate experiences, so that it would be easy for him to live in the moment, and;

2. Adapting particular attention towards one's experiences, which would then help a person become more accepting, open, and curious.

When these work together, the person becomes whole—and so stress no longer would rule over his life.

However, it is not…

…something that you should do to "escape" your life. It is more of connecting with your inner self. In short, it's about getting to know who you are, and not forgetting who you are.

It's also not about what you think, but rather about being self-aware and understanding of what's getting in and out of your head. It's also not about just one kind of experience alone. In fact, there are various mindfulness exercises that you can do—and that's what makes it useful.

Well, you also should keep in mind that mindfulness is not about becoming someone else, and not about becoming "perfect", but rather becoming who you truly are. Mindfulness helps you get into a right place—especially in your mind so you can apply calmness in your life.

And most importantly, mindfulness is not a religious practice. You can be part of any religion and you can enjoy the benefits of mindfulness. As aforementioned, it's really about getting to know yourself more—so you can harness your potential, and maximize its use in your life.

Mindfulness for Beginners

Chapter 2: Why Bother with Mindfulness/ Meditation

Mindfulness, and meditation, in general, are great for you. Why? Well, here are a number of reasons.

1. You'll be able to focus on your senses. You use your senses in your everyday life, but do you actually get to focus on them? Are you able to actually be thankful for them and understand their role in your life? Probably not, right? The key here is to spend just one day in your life trying to be aware of them so that you'll also know how to use them the best way you can.
2. You'll be able to cherish non-verbal experiences. You get to somehow enjoy life without trying to explain things too much. You get to understand that there is a vast world of difference between hearing and listening, or talking and speaking. You get to be a highly spiritual, rather than superficial person.
3. You get to go through your feelings one at a time. Again, it's all about feeling what you need to feel—no matter how good or awful they are.
4. You'll be more content in life—but you'll also realize that you can keep on dreaming and work on those dreams so they could come true.
5. You'll be able to relate to people more and realize that everyone has a battle to fight. That's why you should just help each other out instead of bringing one another down.

6. You'll be more motivated to work or be great at whatever it is that you're doing in life.
7. You'll be a happier individual. You'll feel less alone and you'll realize that you don't have to fight your battles alone anymore.
8. You get to recognize the emotions that you are feeling, and you also get to name them in your mind. For example, after watching a really heartbreaking movie, you start crying. This emotion is called *sadness*. Or, when you see a friend you have not seen in so long and you feel like your heart is bursting with happiness; well, you feel *joy*.
9. You get to accept your emotions, but you do not let them take over your life. See, the problem with some people is that they do not like recognizing emotions. When they're heartbroken, they go out, drink, party—without actually accepting the fact that they're sad and heartbroken, and thus, the healing process takes a long time. When you accept your emotions, you'll notice how easier life can be.
10. You get to become curious about your experiences, and so in turn, you get to investigate them, while feeling different sensations within you.

You see, these things will make you a better, stronger, and definitely happier person.

Chapter 3: It's All in Your Head

Most of the time...it's really all just in your head. But that doesn't make the thoughts less powerful, does it? In fact, because they're in your head, it makes them the most powerful things.

But, in case you have forgotten, you actually have the power to control them. In fact, most of them are just worries. Worries could really drive you mad, even if there is no basis for them—and sometimes, that's really hard.

For example, try answering the following questions:

1. Are you taking care of yourself?

2. Are you worried about something real, or is it all just in your mind?

3. Do you feel overworked?

4. Do you feel underappreciated?

5. Do you really think that this thing you're worrying about will happen, and why?

6. Is there something you can do to prevent the problem from happening, or is it out of your control?

7. What makes you so scared?

8. What situations affect you?

8

9.   Which kind of people makes you anxious?

10. Why exactly are you worried?

Most of the time, the reason why you're so worried is because you have urges. Everyone has urges. It is normal for a person to crave for certain things, and want things that are not always good for him. For example, even if someone is on a diet, he may feel the urge to eat junk foods, or to eat a lot of carbs, even if he's not supposed to. People are susceptible to temptation.

A person's urges could be likened to a wave. Sometimes, that wave surges and it overwhelms you; it surrounds you. According to the late, great psychologist Alan Marlatt, PhD, people often have the urge to switch back to their old habits, no matter how negative those may seem to be. Just like waves, urges also rise in intensity, and you get to feel them enveloping you. And just like waves, you can also surf on your urges and emerge victoriously.

But, remember, your urges are not who you are, and you still have so much control over them. There are basically 4 stages to surfing those urges, and these are:

1.   Acknowledge the urge—and how you experience it.

2.   Focus on a certain part of your body where you feel like you experience the craving the most.

3.   Take a deep breath, and release tension as you do so.

4.   Repeat the focus on the part of your body that sees the craving.

Mindfulness for Beginners

According to Dr. Sarah Bowen of the *Center for the Study of Health and Risk Behaviors* at the *University of Washington*, every person has the capacity to fight his urges in ways that he knows best. People cope via experience, and that's why they have to strengthen their minds so it would be easier to control urges and other things in life.

What you can do then is try to combat those temptations and you can do so by practicing the following:

1. Close your eyes and try to understand where in your body you experience the urges. Just sit somewhere quiet, remember an urge, and then shift attention to where you feel the said urge in your body. Take note that this differs from person to person so you really cannot compare it with others. Just try to find a situation that feels closest to you, and focus on that.

2. Try to picture the said situation as specific as you can in your mind, and then turn your attention back into it.

3. Once you have focused your attention there, get lost in the moment and notice the sensations that you feel. Is there any saturation? Do you feel some kind of tingling sensation? Do you see or feel or sense colors in any way? Be objective and not judgmental. Just because you have recognized something does not mean you have to judge yourself for it.

4. Draw an imaginary outline around the place where you felt the sensation and notice how you feel after doing so.

5. Focus on your breathing, and watch it change in a matter of 1 to 2 minutes. Even if you feel like your breathing patterns have not changed, do not skip this part. You may also try

saying the words "breathe in", and "breathe out" if you think that would make it easier for you to focus.

6. After doing that breathing exercise, focus on the part where you felt the urges again.

7. Again, notice how those parts of your body feel, or if there are certain sensations that you currently feel there. You can breathe in and out again if you feel like it will help, and then watch the sensations change. Try to do this for at least a minute—or longer, if you still can.

8. Now, imagine that your urges are waves, and the sensations you feel are also what you feel while facing a real wave. Try to imagine the wave rising and falling as the sensations inside you reach their peak and then subside.

9. Now, try to use your breath as a means to ride the said waves, and just pretend that you are a pro-surfer and that the wave will not be able to consume you. Try thinking of this for a minute or so; again, the longer, the better.

10. Ride the said wave and think of the sensations in an objective, non-judgmental way. You'll probably feel some warmth in your belly as the sensations increase.

11. Then, after surfing the urge, go ahead and congratulate yourself. Remind yourself that you actually could kick those urges away—especially if you want to.

Chapter 4: Be Mindful of What You Put Into Your Body and Mind

Another thing that you have to keep in mind is that you have to be mindful of what you feed your mind and body. Certain food products (such as too much fat, carbs, or sugar) can make you feel bloated—and of course, that does nothing good for your brain.

Feeding yourself is not just about what you eat, but also about what you tell your mind, and even what you hear, and watch onscreen. The television—and movies, and even books and newspapers are so powerful because you see an image of what's happening. Sometimes, you'd watch TV and see people getting wasted, doing drugs—and somehow, you begin to think it's a "cool thing". Of course, it's still up to you to decide what you want to do with your life, and that's true. But you also have to keep in mind that if you do not surround yourself with positive things, your spirits might be dampened.

Same goes for what you listen to. There are times when you're already so stressed out and you listen to music that's too noisy— probably to let the rage out—or too sad, and guess what? You get to feel the mood of the music. You become sadder, angrier even, and that's not good.

In short, you have to surround yourself with food that could help your mind feel better (such as nuts, apples, apricots, and most vegetables), music that could make you feel good and happy, and shows and books that could inspire you—instead of make you feel like you're a dumb person living in a dumb world.

By doing so, you get to prepare to meditate, and you're also able to help yourself feel better.

Chapter 5: Eat and Drink Slow

Eating and drinking slowly is also important in mindfulness meditation, getting its roots from the Kabbalah. By eating slowly, you not only get to make your metabolic rate faster, but you also get to appreciate what's in front of you. And, you get to prepare yourself for other mindfulness exercises that you'll be doing in the future, too.

Here's what happens: more than anything, when you see and touch the food and beverage (the container of the beverage, of course) in front of you, you can ask yourself how it looks and feels like—and how you feel about it. You will then find yourself slowly coming into a state of bliss—because you get to realize that you actually have something to eat, and that's something you should be grateful for.

Then, you can come back to asking yourself what the food or the beverage reminds you of. What certain point in your life do you remember at the moment? How does the food make you feel inside? Or, does it remind you of a bad time in your life? Does it make you feel nauseated? Why?

Consider everything that came into making that food. Try to think about the people who have made it; its history and the like. How do you think chocolate came about? How is it made? See, by asking these questions, you get to realize that each serving of food that you have is actually special—even if the food doesn't seem like it.

Now, place the food in your mouth. Revel in its taste and the feel of it inside your mouth. Take note of how your body reacts to it—and even your mind. Savor each bite and make sure that you realize how good it is. If you don't like the food, think of why you don't like it—and what makes you feel like it's something you wouldn't want to eat over and over again.

By doing so, you get to appreciate food—and realize how it really is a part of your soul.

Chapter 6: Tips for Beginners

They say that when you put your heart into something, then you'll be able to ace it. The same could be said of mindfulness.

In order to make mindfulness work for you, you have to make sure that you have the following attitudes:

1. **A Beginner's Mind**. Even if you haven't tried mindfulness before and you're not too sure about it, always keep in mind that this experience would be good for you. Have some clamor for it. Be excited about it.
2. **Trust**. If you do not believe in what you're about to embark on, who will? You have to give something your 100%. You have to make sure that you believe it so that your heart would be into it.
3. **Patience**. Mindfulness isn't some kind of miracle. Even medicines take time to work—so make sure that you have patience, and that you keep on doing it. Remember that things would not work if you give up on them right away.
4. **Non-Striving**. Allow yourself to be vulnerable. Allow yourself to feel what you need to feel; to just stay in the moment and just lose yourself in the process of mindfulness. Don't push yourself too hard—you won't be able to enjoy it that way.
5. **Non-judging**. Do not judge whatever you observe. Remember that they're all part of your life and it would not be good for you to be overly critical of them—or of yourself.

This is your chance to let go of what hurts you—not the other way around.

6. **Letting go**. Speaking of letting go, you do have to remind yourself that sometimes, in order to move on in life, you have to let go of the things that hurt. Open your heart and have some courage to let go—you never know how much it'll help.

7. **Kindness**. Be kind to yourself, and to the moment that you're in. Bask in it. Get lost in it. Don't think about anything else—for now, and just enjoy the moment. Bask in everything you feel.

8. **Acceptance**. Just because you accept something doesn't mean you have lost. On the contrary, it means you are actually strong enough to let go of what you can no longer change—and start living a better life.

9. **Curiosity**. Just like Alice when she got lost in Wonderland, allow yourself to enjoy what you're doing, be curious about it, and simply forget the world for a while!

When you respect and understand Mindfulness, it surely will work for you!

Chapter 7: How to Practice Mindfulness

Of course, it's best to start with the basics. In order to perfume basic mindfulness, which is all about calming the mind, and allowing yourself to enter that state of self-awareness and acceptance.

Here's what you could do.

1. Sit down comfortably on a mat or on the floor, and focus on your own sense of breathing. Just breathe; you actually don't have to do deep-breathing, or try to count your breaths and such. Just breathe and focus on how it's happening. Feel it coming through your nose, by your throat, or even in the chest and diaphragm.

2. Feel your breaths. By doing so, you're kept grounded and you get to the point where you see that breathing is actually amazing and that it's something that keeps you alive.

3. Bring your attention back to your breathing. Sometimes, your mind may wander off and it's best to just cut it out and focus on breathing again. Don't criticize yourself, though. Just tell yourself that you're breathing. Focus on that.

You could also try Shamatha Mindfulness, which goes like this:

1. Sit down and tell yourself that at this moment, you are going to work for the betterment of your mind. Sit upright and

make sure that your feet touch the ground. Or sit down on the floor or on a yoga mat with your legs crossed to feel stable and strong.

2. Don't forget to make sure that you are in an erect position and that your shoulders are on the same level with each other.

3. Look down, just a couple of inches from your nose. Make sure that you don't get distracted by looking at other things.

4. Just relax and breathe. Don't think about anything else and focus only on your breathing patterns. Imagine how each breath flows throughout each part of your body.

If any thought comes up, just tell yourself to stop thinking about it because it does not belong at this moment. Focus on that. Afterwards, you could utter the following affirmations:

1. *I am brilliant, and I can do a lot.*

2. *I am the designer of my life. I can always change my life.*

3. *I am happy—and even if there may be hard times, I know that they will pass, too.*

4. *I am a brave person, and I will not let anyone else pull me down, but I also am in charge of choosing my battles.*

5. *I will let go of things that pull me down.*

6. *I am full of grace.*

7. *I'll be able to reach my goals in time.*

8. *In a couple of years, I'll be able to move into a new house, and travel.*

9. *I am on the path to the greatness.*

10. *I'll be able to achieve my dreams.*

Remember to try practicing this daily, and once you get the hang of it, you can move on to other mindfulness exercises. Or, you can also try other meditative exercises as early as now because you might get to focus on them more. Check out the next chapters to see what this means.

Mindfulness for Beginners

Chapter 8: How to Live in the Present

Living in the present is definitely easier said than done. After all, everyone
has a past, and sometimes, that past could really mess up with the present. But here's the thing: by allowing the past to mess up with the present, you kind of get to ruin the future a bit because you keep living in the past. You don't give yourself a chance to be redeemed and forgiven for your past transgressions—even by yourself.

When you don't forgive yourself for your past mistakes, you tend to become someone who feels like the whole world is conspiring against you. There are days when you feel like you've already done your best and yet, nothing good ever happens. Days like these are the worst because you might feel as if you'll never achieve success again.

Well, guess what? You can definitely move past this awful moment in your life and become the kind of person that you have always wanted to become—or maybe even someone better than that.

What needs to be done? Read these tips and find out.

What you have to keep in mind is that you have to assess the situation. You have to ask yourself questions such as:

What could be done to make it better?

What makes you feel bad about the situation?

What went wrong?

By seeing the gravity of the situation and seeing where things went wrong, it would be easy for you to know and understand what you can do to make things right. As they say, you have to face your problems head on instead of ignoring them and trying to escape from them because the more you try to escape, the worse things get.

Then, if you already know what went wrong, you can start planning about what you can do to rise up from the fall. Others write about their plans, make lists, or even make use of cork boards where they can pin write-ups and photos of their plans. In Psychology, it is said that if you can visualize something, it has more premise of coming true. This is because if the mind can see something, it becomes more inclined to achieving it.

For example, you lost some of your savings and then you write about this trip you're supposed to go to. You also write about your plans for making money and saving up again. When you realize that you have all these plans, you'll be more enthusiastic about working or doing whatever you can to save up. Somehow, it makes things easier instead of just wallowing in your situation and doing nothing about it. This way, you can make things right and you are also able to help yourself become a better and stronger person, too.

Chapter 9: How to Become Stress and Anxiety Free

Anxiety could really make you feel bad about yourself and prevent you from mindfully meditating the right way. However, before meditating, you could start addressing your anxiety first so you can work on letting go of it.

As a start, you can answer the following questions:

1. As a child, how did you usually feel when you were around your parents/family?

2. What usually made you feel anxious as a child?

3. Were you very shy as a child? Or, did you notice your shyness showing as you grew up?

4. Have you always had trouble relaxing?

5. What usually runs in your mind?

6. What things are you most worried about?

7. Have you ever felt unloved or underappreciated as a child?

8. Are you often irritated or annoyed?

9. Do you often fear that something terrible might happen?

10. What other symptoms do you feel aside from what's given?

11. What other conditions do you suffer from?

12. Are there particular people you do not want to be around with? Who are they and why?

13. What situations annoy you?

14. What situations make you feel like running away?

15. What provokes you?

16. How do you feel when your routine gets interrupted or when something out of the ordinary happens?

17. How do you feel when someone invites you to a party?

18. Where do you think your anxiety stems from?

Then, separate them into three categories, namely Physical, Behavioral, and Cognitive. For this, you could keep the following in mind:

1. Physical. What were the symptoms that you feel during your panic attacks or during situations that make you anxious? Remember that it differs for everyone, so it's just right that you write down how it is for you. Here's an example:

"Usually, I get headaches and my heart races so fast whenever I'm in a situation that makes me anxious. I have shaky hands and legs, too, and I feel like I'm somewhere else and it makes me scared. I also hate the fact that there's a lot of light around the room."

2. Behavioral. This is about how you acted or tried to escape from the anxious situation. For example:

"I covered my ears with my hands so I wouldn't be able to hear what's going on around me. I also put a blanket over myself so I won't be able to see light because it makes me feel all the more awful. Whenever I have my earphones and my iPod with me, I also just try to listen to music so I won't hear other people."

3. Cognitive. Finally, you have to write down the thoughts you usually have during your attacks.

"I feel like I literally just want to be transported away from the situation—like I want to be anywhere but there. I want the world to swallow me up; I just want to be gone."

And afterwards, you could form positive reactions in your head by means of learning reaction formation, which goes like this:

1. Instead of asking someone to pay for what I have bought at the mall for me, I will do it myself.

2. Instead of saying "no" right away to the person who invited me to a party, I'll say yes and I'll show up. After all, I am not sure of what happens but it could be great and I might meet someone nice.

3. If I'm asked to make a speech or speak in public, I'll make sure that I have prepared for it. I don't have to be perfect but at least, I know that I have prepared and I won't be embarrassed.

4. If people around me are being so noisy, I'd just put some music on and wear my earphones so I won't be able to hear them. Or, maybe, I'll try to join the conversation.

Basically, you have to assess the situation so you could create positive responses in your head. In creating these responses, you need lots of practice but soon, it will pay off.

When you think positively and have positive responses, you'll be able to do it in real life, too. It's not that simple, of course, but just take it a step at a time and you'll be fine.

Chapter 10: How to Make a Plan to Meditate Mindfully

Mindfulness isn't just something you'd do right away. Of course, if you want it to work the right way, you have to plan for it. For this, you can try doing the following:

1. **Set aside a time of your day for it.** When do you practice mindfulness? Would it be great to do it early in the morning? What about after coming home from work? It's important to set a regular time for you to do it each day so that you would not forget. You also have to make sure that you do it only during that time—and that you recognize it as a time to meditate. 5 to 20 minutes each day is already good.

2. **Keep a mindfulness journal.** Write how you have practiced for the day, how you felt, and what you think you should do for the next session. This is a good way of keeping track of your progress, and seeing how mindfulness could work—and is working—for you.

3. **Know the right posture.** What you have to do is make sure that you're comfortable. You could either sit on a chair with your feet firmly planted on the ground, or sit on a mat or medicated cushion. If you can't sit, just lay down—but make sure you wouldn't fall asleep!

4. **Breathe deeply.** Make sure you breathe from your belly so you wouldn't breathe shallowly from the chest.

Once you've got that covered, you could start meditating mindfully daily. You could even make use of various exercises each day—so that the process won't be monotonous—and so you'd actually be able to enjoy the exercises instead of feeling like you're just obligated to do them.

Chapter 11: Letting Go of Your Past

Mindfulness means that you have to stop living in the past, and start living in the present. By doing so, you get to appreciate your life.

For this, you could try understanding what happened in the past, also known as events, so you could understand how you should—or should've—reacted, and what you can make out of it so you'd have a better future. For this, you could do the following:

1. Understand what happened. Various events happen in one's life—it could be anything that makes you feel something inside. It could be a comment of your coworker (Your hair looks different today, You have something in your lips, Your desk is untidy, etc.), the behavior of your partner (he seems off, his eyes seems crossed, etc.), the weather—anything. Now, what you have to do is think about how you usually react in situations like that. Just think or write about it—for now.

2. Understand how you reacted. The next thing you have to do is think about your responses for each situation. For example, when the skies turn dark, you often feel scared. When your partner seems off, you just want to argue with him. When your coworker couldn't keep his comments to himself, you tend to feel so bad about yourself.

You see, the thing is that your responses are actually valid. You react to certain things because they tap something inside you. You responses are actually comprised of your thoughts, emotions, and behavior—which is exactly why people react to things in different ways.

For example, if you've had such a rough life, even the littlest things could make you feel so bad about yourself—and make you depressed. But remember, every second that you spend depressed is another second you would not be able to get back. When you let the world win, you're letting yourself lose—is that what you want?

3. **Understand what you can make out of it, and what you can take from it.** Now, it's time for you to change your response. When your co-worker comments on your hair, thank her about it—and she just might feel like she was burned. You have the choice whether to be affected by someone's comments or not, and you know what? It's best for you to turn it around. When you shape your responses, you shape the outcome of what your life would be. Instead of getting bummed by those comments, you get to feel better about yourself—and work the best way you could!

Chapter 12: Take Small Steps in the Right Direction, Everyday

Making Mindfulness a part of your life means that you have to incorporate it into your everyday life. As they say, small steps could really lead to big and great things, and in this case, you could try doing the following:

1. **Communicating Mindfully** Try to be aware of the sound of your own voice as you speak with someone else. Also, try to be aware of how the voice of the person you're talking to sounds like. Make sure not to criticize but to just get back in the moment. What matters is you notice the difference in your tones.

2. **Exercising Mindfully.** Be mindful of what's going on around you while you're working out. Focus attention on what you feel in your body as you run or as you do crunches and the like. Focus your thoughts on how your body reacts to what you're doing, so that you'd understand why it's great for you to exercise, and why it actually matters.

3. **Vacationing Mindfully.** When you're on holiday, stop thinking about the life you have to get back to, or the next holiday you're going to take. Instead, shift your focus on the given moment. Enjoy the feeling of the sun on your skin, the sand in your toes, and the fresh air around you. Be thankful for where you are at the moment. Bask in it. Allow it to enter every part of your soul.

4. **Musical Mindfulness.** Listen to your favorite song or the song you cannot stop listening to right now, and then just listen to it. Don't just listen to the words—listen to the beat itself. Listen to both of them and think about how words and music bring a song together.

5. **Waiting Mindfully.** Whenever you feel frustrated while waiting in line for a cab, or while lining up in a shop, notice the things around you. What are the colors that you see? Notice how you feel. If you feel frustrated, acknowledge it, but do not let it consume you. Think of this as an exercise that you're doing to keep yourself in check while in something that you cannot control. Try to focus on your breathing so you'd also be able to calm down. This way, instead of being annoyed, you'd realize that waiting is just a normal part of life—and there is nothing wrong with it.

6. **Walking Mindfully.** Try to notice the sensations between your feet and the ground as you walk towards where you're going. Once you are doing this, you'll probably feel like your weight is actually shifting from one foot to the other. Try to get lost in that moment, and to just feel all that you can feel around you: the smell of the flowers, the feel of the wind on your hair, the feeling of sweat in your skin, etc.

7. **Working Mindfully.** Yes, it's often hard to appreciate work, but hey, without it, you might not be able to pay the bills. The key here is to understand that you are there because you are supposed to be there. The fact that there's a job handed to you means that you're actually doing something good for the benefit of others. Try to be attentive to your work. By knowing that people actually appreciate what you do, even without saying it out loud, you'll be able

to push yourself to work harder and better. This way, you wouldn't have to exert a lot of effort and things would be more natural.

It is also said that allowing yourself to learn new things is an act of mindfulness because you're opening yourself up to a different world. The act of forgiving and accepting others is important, too.

Chapter 13: Be Present, Compassionate, and Grateful When Talking to Others

When you're talking to other people, you also have to be able to apply mindfulness. By doing so, you're really able to understand what the other person is trying to say, and you get to know yourself more, too.

For this, it would be good to practice non-verbal skills. These will all keep you in the present—and will make you a better conversationalist. For this, you can do the following:

1. Always lean forward and keep your head up.

2. Ask help from a friend to watch you while you practice so he could also provide you with the comments that you need.

3. Make sure not to cross your arms.

4. Make sure that you try to practice one skill at a time so that you wouldn't be overwhelmed and you would still be natural.

5. Make sure to smile warmly and make appropriate eye contact while talking.

6. Once you're confident enough, try it out in real-life situations.

7. Stand close when talking to others so you could make them feel like you're inviting them to your world, and you have no problem being invited in theirs.

8. Try practicing in front of a mirror. This will help you see what you need to change or improve right away.

9. Watch your tone of voice. Make it clear and confident—but never arrogant.

Chapter 14: Let Go of Distractions

Practicing mindfulness also means that you have to start letting go of distractions.

Distractions are just temptations, and you know what happened when Eve bit that fruit. They only keep you away from what you're supposed to be, and how you're supposed to feel. Basically, if you learn how to let go of things that distract you, even for just a while, you'll be able to concentrate on what you're supposed to do. Here are some suggestions:

1. Take some time out from social media. Sometimes, what you see online may just irritate you which will lead to not being able to finish your task right away. Being away from social media, even for just a day or so, would already make you feel a lot better about yourself, and would make you realize how great life actually is.

2. Don't eat while working, especially if you're not hungry. Sometimes, food becomes so much like your comfort object— and that's not a good thing. You have to eat when it's time—and not all the time.

3. Stop thinking of that movie you're going to watch if you still have some work to finish. Focus on the now.

Mindfulness for Beginners

Chapter 15: Mindfulness at Home and Work

And of course, when you're at home and at the office, you can also make use of mindfulness so that you would be in a good place. For this, you can try the following:

1. While doing household chores, try to focus on how you feel. For example, how does water and soap feel on your hands while washing the dishes? How much do you like aligning frames, or using wallpaper?

2. What is the natural taste in your mouth when you are not eating? How does it taste like?

3. Walk around the house or your room with your eyes closed, and then just try to lose yourself in the scents you smell.

4. Turn on the radio while in a quiet room and get it down to the lowest volume. This way, you'd be able to listen to it as carefully and as intently as you could. You could also turn it on, put it in a normal volume, and go around the house without losing focus on the radio.

5. Try to see whether certain flavors affect your mood. Compare the feeling of eating chocolate to barbecue, apples to oranges, etc.

6. Try to eat or taste something that you absolutely hate. Remember not to say that you do not like it or that it is bad, and just focus on the taste and the feeling that you get while eating it.

7. Touch skin on various parts of your body, and see how your body reacts to each touch. Tickle, scratch (lightly), rub, and do other things on your skin, and notice texture, vitality, oiliness, or how there is hair or not.

8. Touch objects with various kinds of temperatures. For example, cold water, a popsicle, a hot mug, etc. See how you'd react to each of them.

9. Touch objects not only with your hands but also with other parts of the body, such as your feet, your knees, your lips, your ears, your nose, etc. Then, see how you feel as each part of your body touches various objects.

10. Touch furniture and other objects in the house and lose yourself in how each of them feels.

11. Taste different foods and see how your food receptors (sweetness, saltiness, sourness, bitterness) work. Which one is most prevalent?

12. Tap objects around the house with the use of a spoon and then try to focus on the sounds that it generates.

13. Smell various kinds of scents at home: perfumes, cleaners, medicine, spices, herbs, condiments, juices, food, etc.

14. Smell something unpleasant—and then just try to focus on the scent, without judgment, and try to understand why it smells that way. Compare spoiled food with cat poop, etc.

15. Small a fragrance and see how you'd react to it. Does it make you feel dizzy? Does it remind you of a certain time in your life? Does it make you happy? Feel those.

16. Place food in your mouth and leave it there for a couple of seconds. Try to explore or understand flavors as the food moves around your mouth. Bite, and see if you can detect any changes.

17. Pinch your nose with one hand while eating a spoonful of food, release, and then eat another spoonful. How do you feel? What is the difference between the two?

18. Look for a song that uses more than one instrument and listen to it intently. Try to separate the various instruments from one another. Notice how rhythm changes, and how the various instruments make the song a whole.

19. Look for a metal object, try to strike it, and find that slashing, banging sound. Listen to how the sound progresses and how it ends.

20. Listen to whatever's going on around you right now. Is some music playing? Do you hear the sounds of a reality show on television? Are some kids around? Do you hear birds chirping? Get lost in the moment and try not to label what you hear as "noise" but as plain sounds.

21. Listen to the sounds that your body makes by putting a hand over one ear. Good examples would be the grumbling of your stomach, your heartbeat, your breathing, etc.

22. Listen to music and see how your body responds to it. How do you feel like your muscles are reacting to it? Do they relax, or do they tighten? Do you feel like dancing, or does what you hear irritate you? Just try to see how your body responds.

23. Let your fingers "explore" the various items you have at home, and see how you'd feel about that.

24. Do household chores and listen to the sounds they create. (i.e., the sounds of the washing machine, how the broom sounds when it sweeps things around, etc.)

25. Collect various kinds of objects and fabric. (I,e., fur, nylon, velvet, plastic, steel, etc.) Feel how each texture feels, and see how you'd react to them. What do you like best? What makes you feel queasy? What makes you feel great?

26. Clean items you have at home and try to "taste" them. (i.e., pen, crystal, keys, cards, etc.) How do each of them "taste" like, or feel?

See? It's not that hard, and now, you'd be able to appreciate whatever's going on around you even more!

Conclusion

I hope this book was able to help you to learn a thing or two about Mindfulness—and how you can practice it in your everyday life.

In order to make sure that you'd be able to practice and imbibe mindfulness each day, make sure that you do the following:

1. Set aside time for it;

2. Feed your mind and body the right way;

3. Appreciate what you have around you;

4. Manage your worries—and fight anxiety;

5. Live in the moment;

6. Take small steps each day, and;

7. Practice mindfulness at home and at work.

By doing so, you'd surely get to live a stress-free, happy life! Finally, if you enjoyed this book, then I'd like to ask you for a favor, would you be kind enough to leave a honest review for this book on Amazon? It would help other people to find out if this book is something that could help them on their journey to a peaceful life. **It would also be greatly appreciated.**

Thank you and good luck!

Preview Of Chakras For Beginners: How to Awaken And Balance Chakras, Radiate Positive Energy And Heal Yourself

Introduction

This book contains steps and strategies on how to awaken your chakras, how to balance these energies emanating from the chakra points in your body, and how to use this knowledge to make your life better.

For over a thousand years, many people have been interested in psychic studies, not only for paranormal pursuits but for health benefits as well. Knowing your chakra points will definitely give you an edge in balancing your life, making better decisions, and generally living a healthier life; the gift of seeing and feeling these chakra points in action is a bonus.

Energy radiates from our chakras. When you are happy or angry, psychics would be able to see a colored light surrounding you. The color may be red, blue, or white, depending on the emotions you feel that day. The stronger the emotions you feel, the stronger the light would be. On the other hand, your chakra points may also weaken, especially if you have an illness. This is why you can use crystals or gemstones for healing. You actually place them on your chakra points and the positive energy carried by the crystals would then be transferred to the chakra points.

Ultimately, the chakra points are the basis for any other psychic link and activity. For instance, a person with an active third eye (otherwise known as the sixth sense) has the crown chakra working properly and actively, too. People who could read auras would be able to see the purple light coming atop your head and enveloping your whole body. Thus, it is important to note the different chakra points in the body and how you could balance the energy coming from them.

This book will teach you exactly that. This gem contains all the things that you need to know about chakras – the chakra points, the strengths and weaknesses of each point, the colors, notes and gemstones that you can equip yourself with, and more importantly, how to awaken and balance your chakras so that one point is not overpowered by the other. Learn real stuff from this book and see how you can manifest and radiate positive energy through your chakras.

Chapter 1: Chakras and You

A knowledge of chakras and how you can strengthen them is vital for your overall physical, mental, and spiritual health. Chakras are typically defined as the (sometimes) invisible force fields around you, which emanate positive or negative energies depending on your mood, emotions, and health status.

The history of chakras goes a long way. Starting in the 7th century BCE, the Hindus have produced texts linking the deities, religious canon, and the knowledge of these psychic force fields. During this time, the Hindus recorded and wrote the Upanishads – the tome of sacred texts that contained the beliefs of Hindus. Aside from learning about karma and reincarnation, practitioners and then readers of the Upanishads knew that the body had various energy points. Moreover, it claimed that the soul settled in different parts of the body.

The Brahma Upanishads, for instance, taught Hindus that there are four important places in the body where the soul resides: the head, throat, heart, and the navel. Further, the texts stated that your waking consciousness is found in the navel; dreamless sleep is found in the heart; dreaming is found in the throat; and the transcendent state is in the head.

The Yogatattva Upanishads, on the other hand, said that the body parts are associated with the elements of fire, air, water, earth, and ether. It is clear that even in the sacred texts, the body is described to coexist with psychic elements. Thus, the body is not simply a vessel, but it is an extension of the world's energies.
Anyone who has seen auras would say that these auras have colors and different vibrations. Where they come from – the chakra points – also influence the kind of auras that people see in you. If you feel very happy or excited, your aura will manifest the energy that you feel; such energy can even be transferred to other people. Have you ever walked in a room full of angry

people, only to leave the same room feeling angry yourself? That is aura and energy at work. You somehow absorb the energy, whether positive or negative, emanating from other people.

The way you feel also affects your health. Scientific studies prove that feeling sorrowful and depressed can be linked to serious illnesses such as fatigue, cancer, and heart problems. Joyous people may have illnesses, too, but these may not be as serious or fatal as what perpetually sad people have.

The work of the chakras is evident here. When your chakras are active and balanced, you would be able to manifest positive energy and vibrantly colored auras. Your moods are uplifted and you feel happy all the time. You don't feel pain or any illness. The more awakened and balanced your chakras are, the better it would be for your body.

Knowing how chakras work is beneficial to your emotional health as well. Imbalanced chakras are like imbalanced hormones. You feel weak, and you don't
have much control over your emotions. When you know how to deal with your chakra points and use other psychic forms of self-healing, your emotional state will be much better. You wouldn't have mood swings; instead, you will immediately be able to block negative forces and emotional baggage that would try to pull you down.

The Seven Chakras of your Body

The word chakra means "wheel of light". This is true, because when people see your aura, they see lights in different colors cocooning you. These chakras are conduits of earth and cosmic energies and connect all the seven layers of your aura. There are energies that come forth from the chakra points.

The chakra points are connected to the various parts of the body. They also have a variety of states, depending on the flow of energy in your body. Chakras may be open, blocked, or sealed. Open chakras radiate more energy. As such, your body becomes more sensitive and receptive to healing and balancing. During the beginning of a healing session, whether it is through acupuncture, crystal healing, or reiki, your chakra points must be open to the energies that will be transferred to you.

In contrast, there are chakras that are sealed. This means that there is a layer that protects your chakras. This is healthy, too, because the layers prevent negative forces from coming in. Think of this as a mantra for some people. Whenever they don't want to feel down or angry, they say a mantra to quickly protect themselves from being influenced by outside forces. They say affirmations like "I will be happy today" or "I can feel that my day will be alright". This is a form of meditation and a way to seal your chakra points.

Chakras may also be blocked, meaning energy is not flowing properly in one point. Blocked chakras affect other chakra points and cause imbalance. Thus, it is important that you have your chakras opened during your meditative state.

A balanced and healthy chakra will be able to radiate positive energy, and the right amount of energy at that. The energy flows freely, but it will not overpower and block your other chakra points. The point of this book is to teach you how to awaken your chakras and manage them to prevent any imbalance of energy in your body.

As aforementioned, there are seven chakras in your body. These chakra points help you in different aspects – physical health, emotions, psychic abilities, etc. These chakras are:

The Earth Star Chakra

The earth star connects you to the elemental energies of the earth. It helps to anchor you to the earth plane so you will be more grounded and logical. Though you acknowledge yourself as a Being of the Light, you have to ground yourself, too, to avoid any misguided feelings. You also need to be grounded so that you could participate in your present embodiment. It helps you remember your highest path in life, your highest affirmations.

The earth star chakra is located beneath your feet. The colors associated with the
earth star chakra are silver, black, and maroon. Naturally, you could choose gemstones and crystals with these colors to aid you in your psychic healing. These stones are onyx, hematite, tiger's eye, and garnet. In terms of psychic ability, you will know how to ground yourself and align yourself with the wonderful powers of the earth.

The good thing about strengthening your earth star chakra is that you become conscious of your being and that you know you are a spirit manifesting itself on the physical plane. You will display a passion and zest for life, and you know how to detach yourself from the chains of the past and the uncertainties of the future. The shadows or weaknesses related to the earth star chakra are depression or disconnection from relationships, lack of motivation to do your activities, and disorders associated with immunity. Hence, you need to activate your earth star chakra to protect yourself from getting anxious and lazy.

The Root Chakra

The root chakra is the source of your usable physical energy and anchors this energy into your physical manifestation. This region is in charge of family and survival issues, relationships, especially within a group. It is the foundation for all the aspects and qualities of your physical being. It is located at the base of your spine that spirals towards the earth star chakra. The color linked to it is red, and the element is earth. In music, the note related to the root chakra is G below the middle C.

When the root chakra is strong, your abilities to touch and smell are strong as well. Likewise, you become clairsentient. Your olfactory senses also work as a psychic ability. This means you can smell and feel unseen entities while others who are not that sensitive and whose root chakras aren't active wouldn't be able to notice any difference in the ambiance of a place.

To complement the energies coming from your root chakra, it is best to wear or bring the following gemstones for protection, healing, and extra motivation: ruby, bloodstone, smoky quartz, obsidian, tourmaline, garnet, red jasper, and red quartz. Naturally, the colors that you have to look for are red and black.

Your root chakra is also responsible for the healing of your skeletal system and circulatory system, your bladder, kidneys, rectum, hips, adrenal gland, skin, feet, and legs. When used properly, the root chakra will help you understand that all things are connected. You become more grounded and stronger when facing uncertainty. You also feel that you belong to a certain place or group. You are more secure and nurturing, channeling the Mother archetype.

When you feel an imbalance in the energy, you feel like giving up and unable to cope. You also feel that you want to detach yourself from a group. You exclude others and you adopt a superior stance. You also channel the Victim archetype and tend to think that everyone is against you. You also feel so insecure.

Go to Amazon.com and check out the rest of the book *"Chakras For Beginners:* How to Awaken And Balance Chakras, Radiate Positive Energy And Heal Yourself".

Check Out My Other Books

Below you'll find my other popular book that is popular on Amazon and Kindle as well. Simply search on the name below on Amazon.com to check them out. Alternatively, you can visit my author page on Amazon (Michael Williams) to see other work done by me.

Chakras For Beginners:

How to Awaken And Balance Chakras, Radiate Positive Energy And Heal Yourself

Buddhism For Beginners:

How To Go From Beginner To Monk And Master Your Mind

Yoga For Men:

Beginner's Step by Step Guide to a Stronger Body & Sharper Mind

Printed in Great Britain
by Amazon